HABITS OF A SUCCESSFUL MIDDLE LEVEL STRING MUSICIAN

VIOLIN

CHRISTOPHER SELBY
SCOTT RUSH

GIA Publications, Inc.
Chicago

Welcome to *Habits of a Successful Middle Level String Musician*. This method book was written to help string players establish an effective daily routine that ultimately leads to great music making. While practicing the various components of playing, remember that improved technique only serves to increase the *artistry* of a musical performance.

This book begins with studies on tone production, bowing, and articulation (right hand), followed by finger patterns and shifting (left hand). Subsequent studies for scales, chorales, rhythm and sight-reading make this a complete method for the advancing string musician. Each exercise has a very specific purpose that leads logically to the performance of concert music. Turn your rehearsal room or practice room into a laboratory for making music, and let your musical journey begin!

Contents:

Tips for Individual Practice:

- Listen to a recording of your favorite artist on your instrument; then imitate that artist's sound.
- Remind yourself why you are practicing. Set goals for each practice session and devise a logical order of things to learn. Strive to cover as many Components of Playing as possible, starting with tone production (bowing variations) and then finger pattern study and scales.
- Begin practice sessions with stretching. *Stay relaxed*—tension is a performer's worst enemy.
- Practice with a mirror. Review basic technique for standing or sitting well, and use left- and right-hand calisthenics to develop relaxed, healthy positions for holding the bow and instrument well.
- Stay focused and rest five minutes for every twenty minutes of practice; unfocused practice is a waste of time and energy and is detrimental to a performer's progress.
- When practicing the sight-reading exercises in the back of the book, use a metronome and establish a slow, reasonable tempo that will allow you to play the exercises with a steady pulse.
- Record yourself and use the recording to identify personal goals for improving your skills and performance.
- Finish your practice session by playing something fun. We practice so we can improve the performance skills needed to express the musical ideas that we find so enjoyable and deeply rewarding.

Habits of a Successful Middle Level String Musician – Violin Edition
Christopher Selby and Scott Rush

G-9601
ISBN: 978-1-62277-275-9

7404 S. Mason Avenue, Chicago, IL 60638
www.giamusic.com

I Tone and Articulation

Open String Exercises

1. Even Tone - Frog to Tip

With a flawless bow hold, play the open string without counting or keeping time; pay attention to the bow's contact point, angle, weight, and speed.

2. Even Bow Distribution

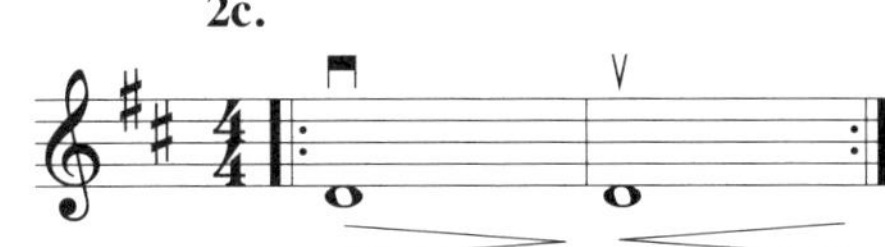

3. Dynamics and Steady Tempo (practice without dynamics first)

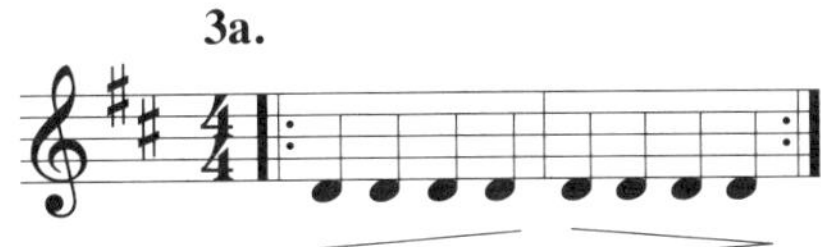

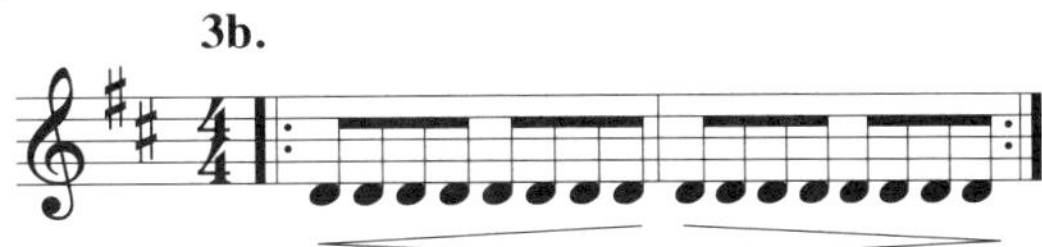

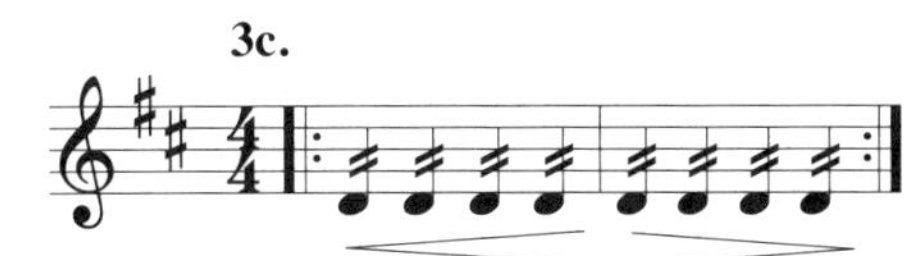

4. Grab and Release

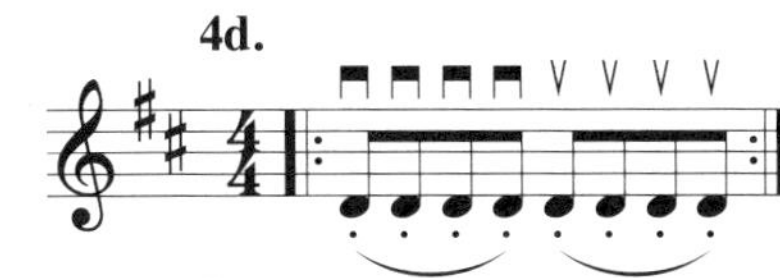

Grab the string then release, allowing string to vibrate—no crunch.

5. String Crossings

6. String Crossing Etude

String Crossing Variations

Bowing Variations

12. Double Stops (First use normal bowing—down, up—then learn to make a good, non-scratchy tone with all down bows.)

13. Spiccato Exercises

Perform the spiccato stroke at the balance point; keep the thumb and pinky curved and the knuckles soft and fluid. Set the bow on the string during the eighth rests.

14. Triplet Bowing Etude and Variations

15. Sixteenth Notes and Slurs

Slurring Variations (for the single 16th note line above)

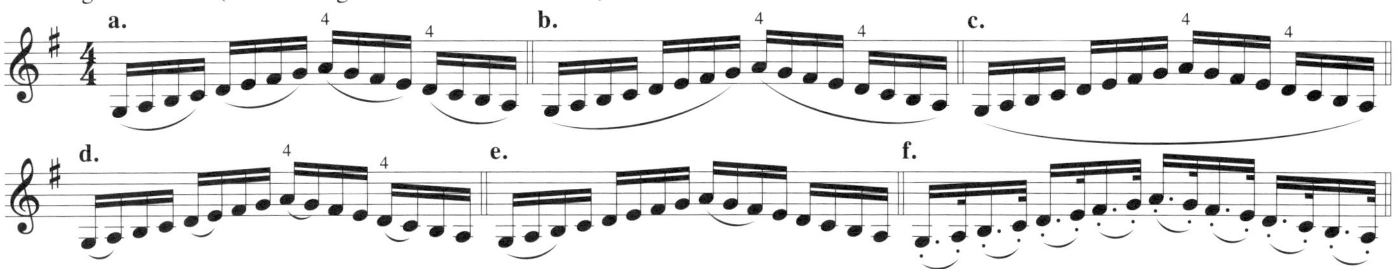

II Finger Pattern Studies

16. First Two Finger Patterns

17. Velocity Drill #1

18. Finger Pattern Drill #1: Natural & Sharp

19. Bourrée

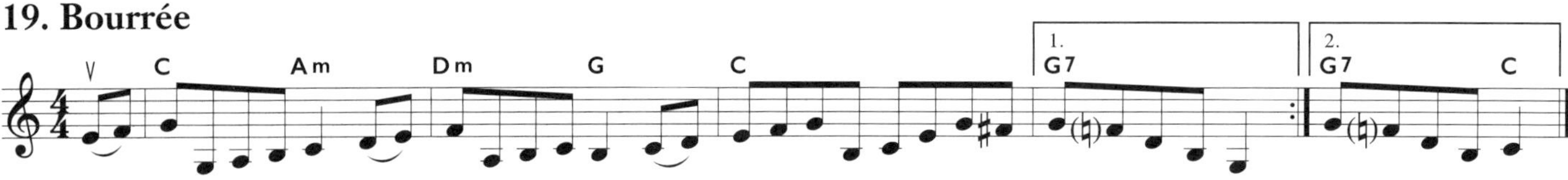

20. Velocity Drill #2

21. Lowcountry Loure

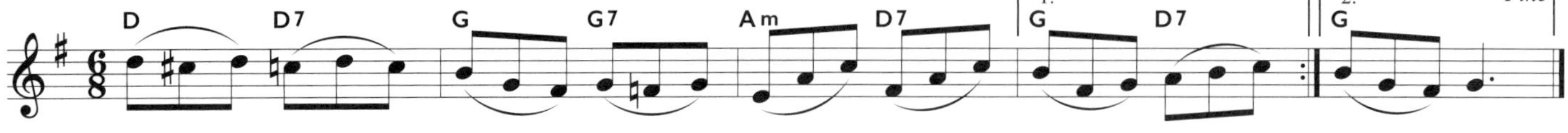

22. Finger Pattern #3

Low 1st finger

23. Finger Pattern Drill #2: Back and Forth
a.
b.
c.
d.
24. Largo from the "New World Symphony"
Dvořák
25. Wide Open Spaces
26. Minor Progression
27. Largo Lamentoso
28. Carolina Reel
Fine
D.C. al Fine
29. Dominant Etude ♩ = 72

30. Preparing for Pattern #4
a.
b.
c.
d.
31. Finger Pattern #4
High 3rd finger
32. Sunrise Salute
33. Major Progression
34. Finger Pattern Drill #4
a.
b.
c.
d.
35. Position Etude in 1st Position
36. Velocity Drill #3
37. Allegro in A Major
A
A7
D
A
E7
A7
1.
Bm
E7
2.
Bm
E
A
Fine
F♯m
Bm
E7
C♯m
F♯m
Bm
E
E7
D.C. al Fine

38. Velocity Etude

First, perform the exercise as written, and then perform with the different finger patterns (#2. C♮ and #3. B♭) shown below.

Finger Patterns

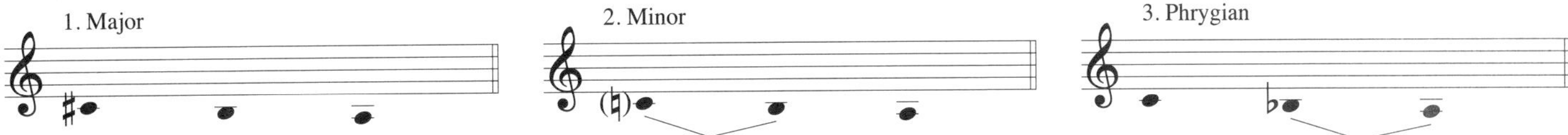

Velocity Etude Variations

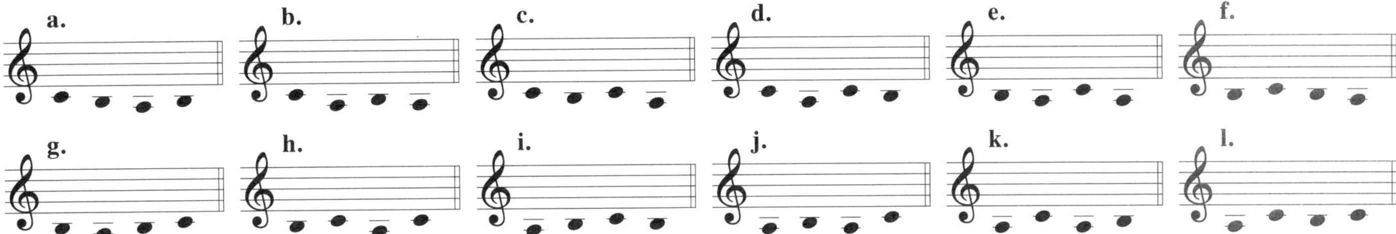

39. Velocity Review and Test

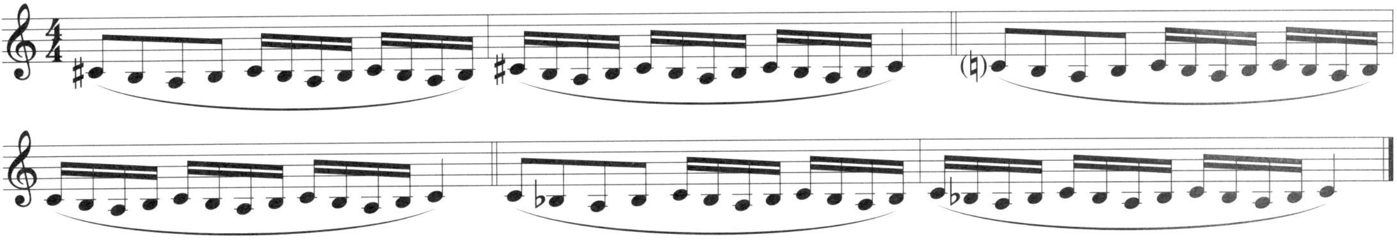

40. Tetrachord Etude

Perform the Tetrachord Etude as written first. Then, perform it with one of the other tetrachord finger patterns below.

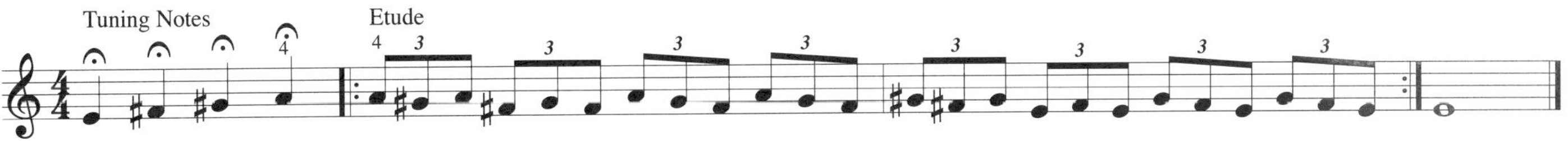

Tetrachords

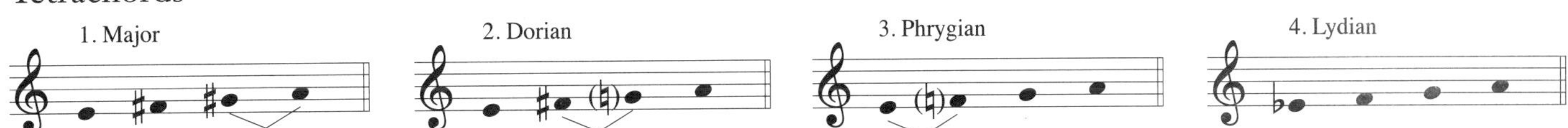

41. Tetrachord Review and Test

Continue the etude using the other finger patterns.

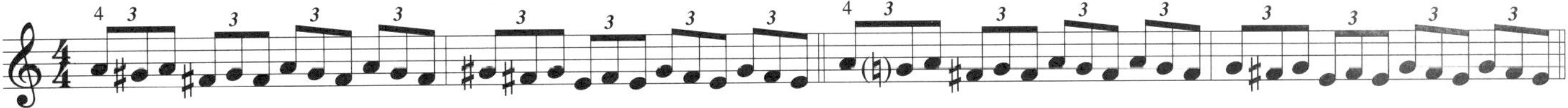

42. Finger Pattern #5

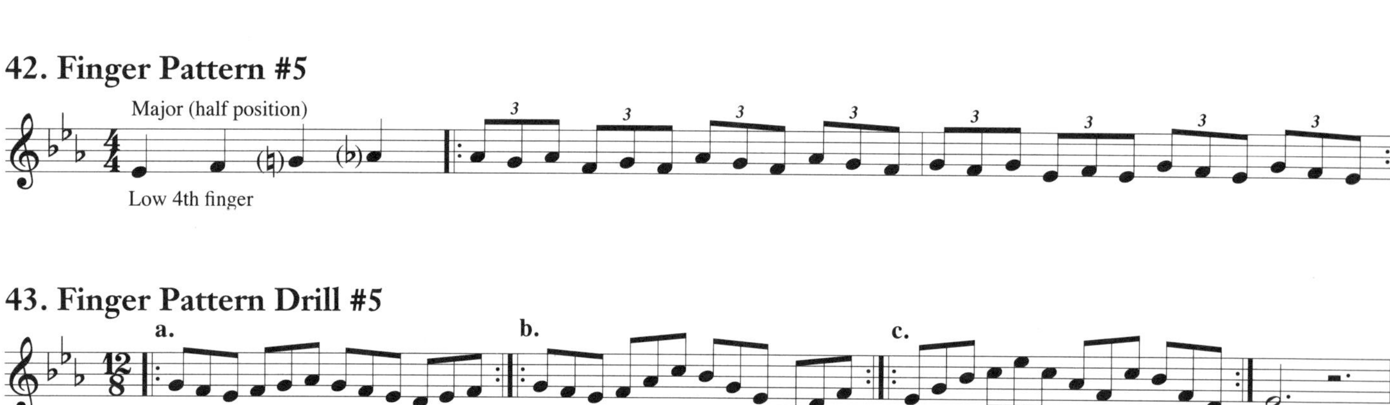

43. Finger Pattern Drill #5

44. Over the Highlands

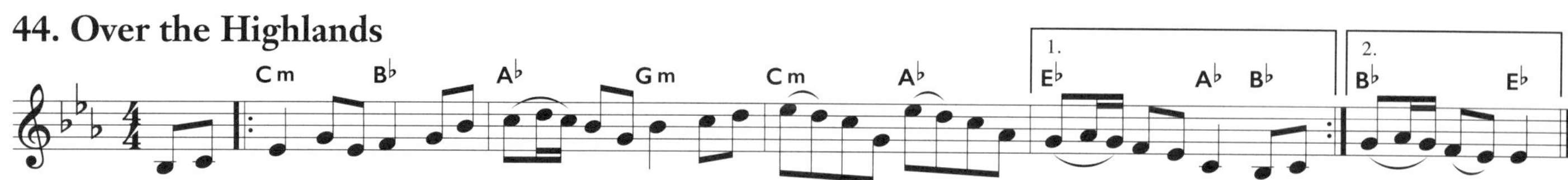

45. Crossing Strings in Flats

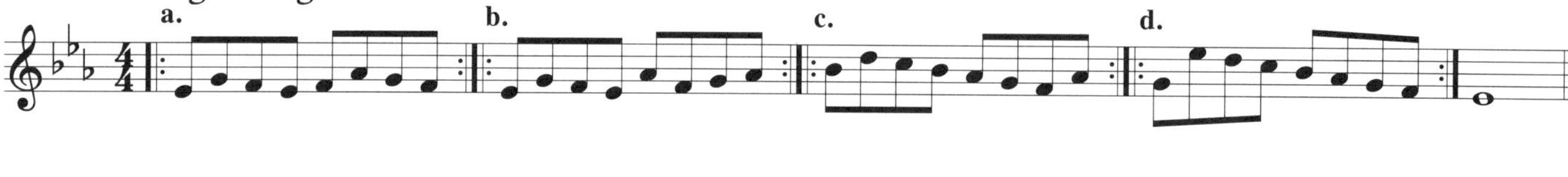

46. E-Flat Folly

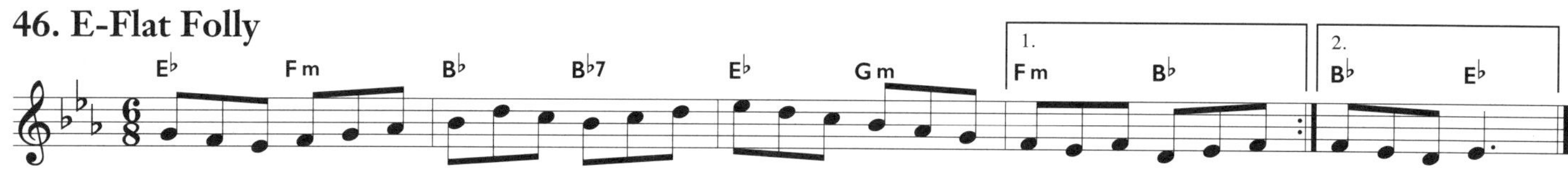

47. Finger Pattern #6

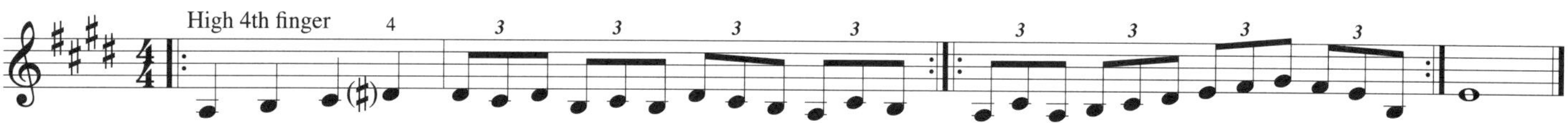

48. Deja Vu: Crossing Strings in Sharps

49. Half Position Drill

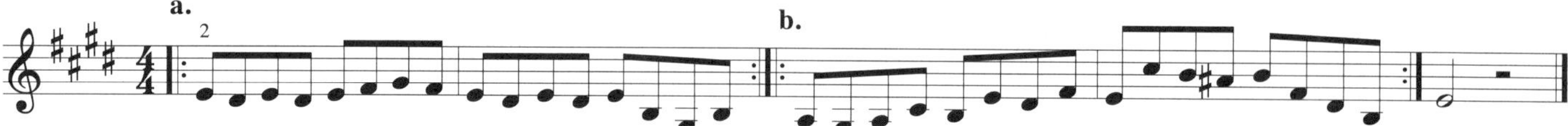

50. Hornpipe

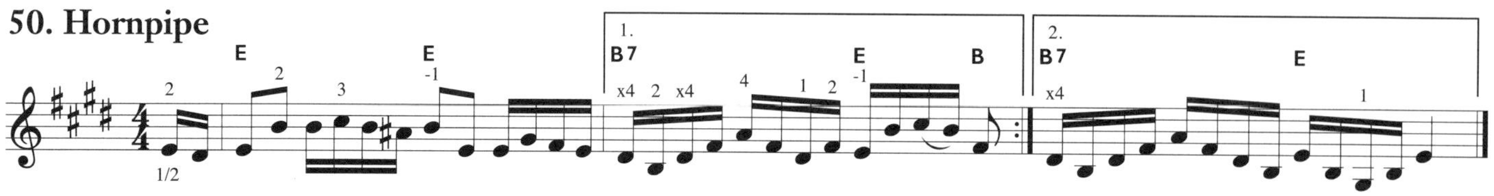

51. Chromatic Fingering Drill

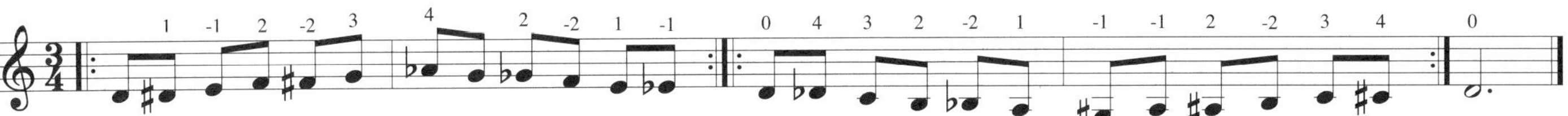

52. Two-Octave Chromatic Scale

53. Introducing Trills

The trills on beats two and four are performed the same way.

54. Trill Drill

55. Through the Keys: A Cumulative Study of Lower Position Patterns

III Shifting and Position Studies

Shift with a light, smooth motion; always move the thumb with the second finger.

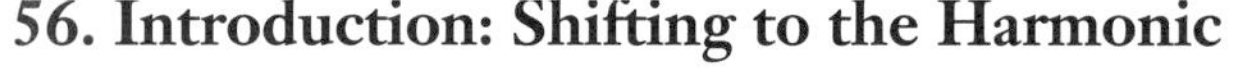

56. Introduction: Shifting to the Harmonic

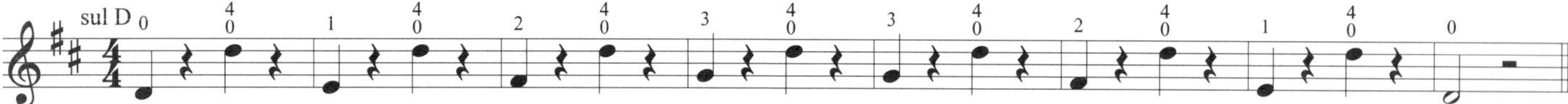

57. Shifting to 3rd Position

58. Shifting to the Same Finger

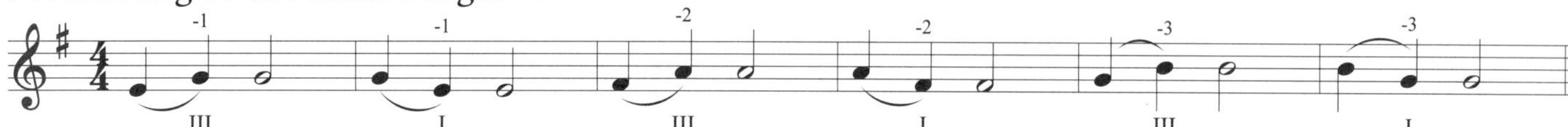

59. Position Drill #1

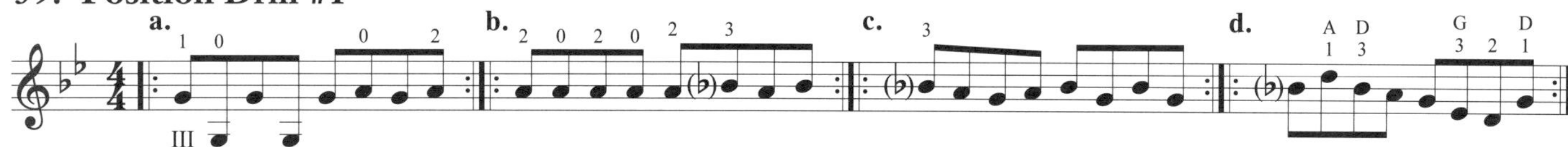

60. The Forgotten Temple

In Part III. Shifting, the letters over the finger number refer to the string on which the note is played.

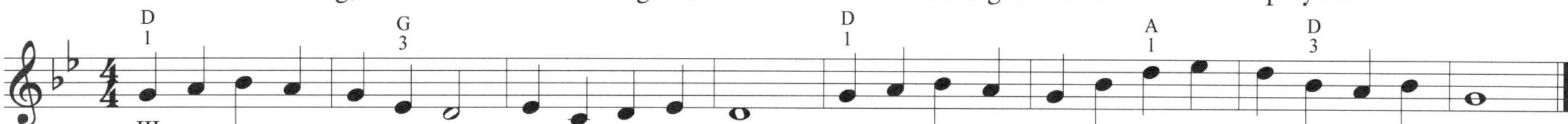

61. Position Drill #2

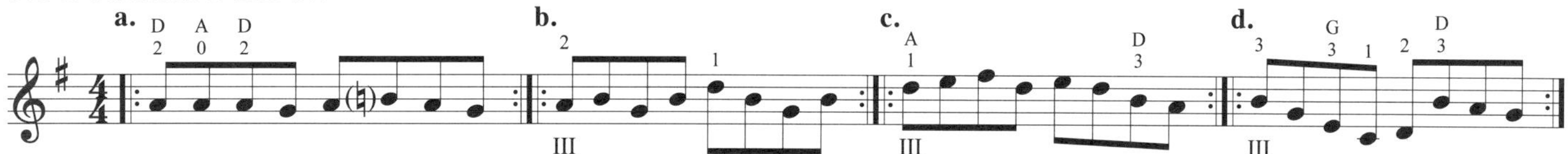

62. Sunrise Salute

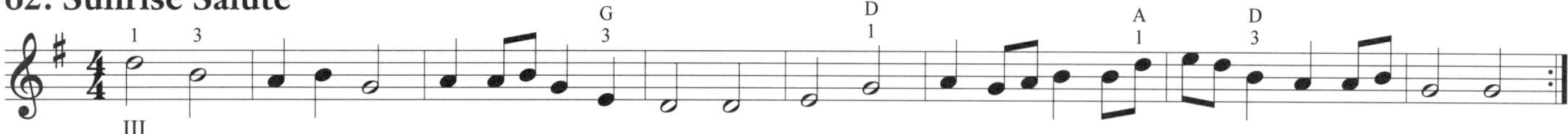

63. Tetrachord Etude (from the note G)

64. Position Drill #3

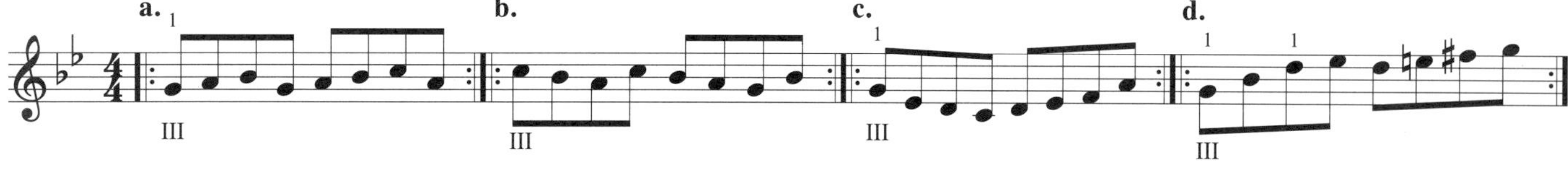

65. Moonlight Minuet
66. Position Drill #4
a. b. c. d.
67. Position Etude in 3rd Position
68. Shifting In and Out of First Position
a. b. c. d.
69. Toy Soldier March
70. Shifting to a Different Finger
a. b. c. d.
71. Misty Mountain
72. Shifting Drill #1
a. b. c. d.
73. Shifting Etude #1
74. Shifting Drill #2
a. b. c. d.

75. Giga Giocoso
76. Shifting Drill #3: Flat Patterns
77. Shifting Etude #2
78. Hilly Flats
79. Silent Shifting #1
The diamond is the destination of the shifting finger; it is a silent shifting note that should be hidden, not heard.
80. Silent Shifting #2
81. Silent Shifting Etude
82. Windy Waltz
Mark the silent shifting notes with a dot or diamond.
83. Silent Shifting #3
84. Shifting Etude #3
Mark the silent shifts with a dot or diamond
85. Shifting to 4th Position

86. Focus on 4th Position

87. Navigating the High C's

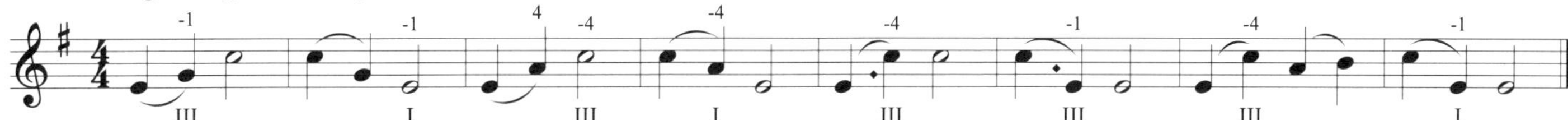

88. Introducing 2nd Position

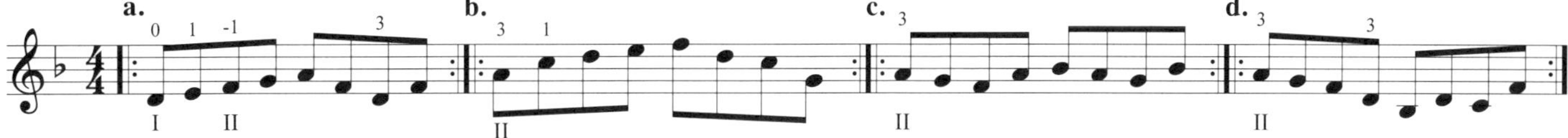

89. Position Etude: 2nd Position

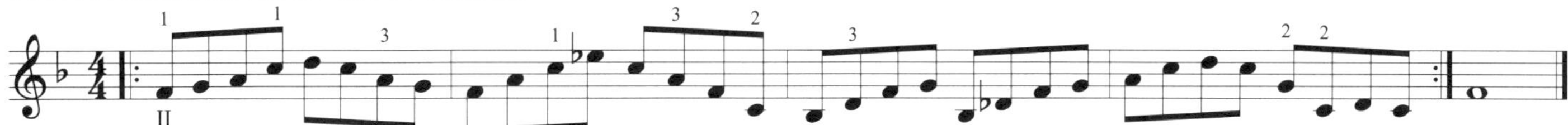

90. Shifting Etude #4

91. D Major Scale and Arpeggio on One String

92. D Minor Scale and Arpeggio on One String

93. Shifting Etude #5

94. Position Etude: 4th Position

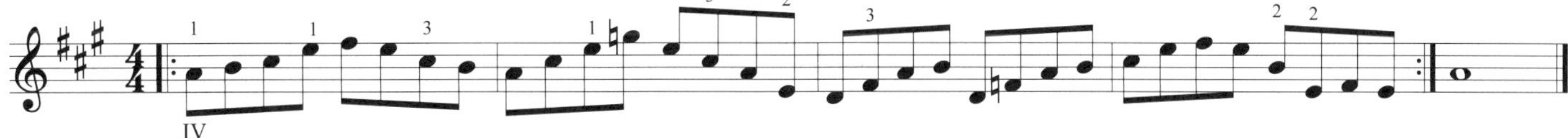

95. Shifting to a Different String

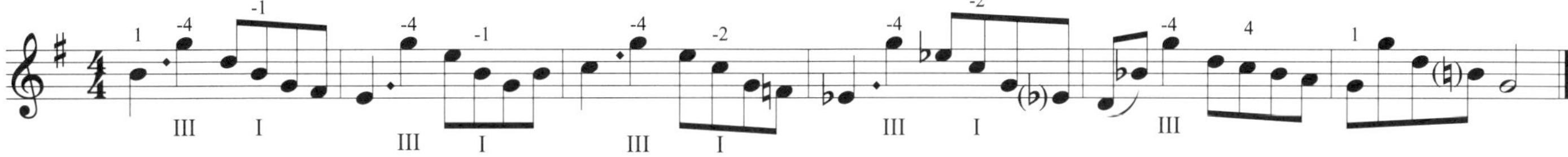

96. Shifting Drill #4: String Crossings and Flats
a.
b.
c.
d.
97. E-Flat Etude
98. Shifting Etude #6 (Finger Replacement and Shifting Across Strings)
99. My Second Home
Fine
D.C. al Fine
100. E-Flat Major Scale and Arpeggio (on one string)
101. E Minor Scale and Arpeggio (on one string)
102. 5th Position Drill
103. Position Etude: 5th Position

IV Scales, Arpeggios and Thirds

Finger Pattern Changes

Each key has a finger pattern that makes it unique. In the key of C, for example, the F-natural feels low, especially when compared to the B-natural that feels high. The gray notes outside of the circle are the notes that do not occur in the key. To understand the entire scale, a complete scale image is included at the bottom of every scale page. The C Major and A Minor scales are shown below.

C Major Scale

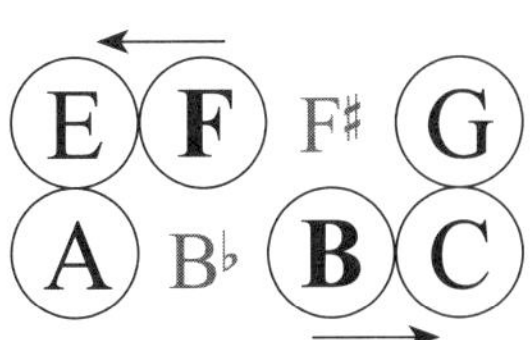

C Major Scale

scale	C	C♯/D♭	D	D♯/E♭	E	**F**	F♯/G♭	G	G♯/A♭	A	A♯/B♭	**B**	C
degree	1	—	2	—	3	**4** ←	—	5	—	6	—	**7** →	1

A Minor Scale

scale	A	A♯/B♭	B	**C♮**	C♯/D♭	D	D♯/E♭	E	**F♮**	F♯/G♭	G	G♯/A♭	A
degree	1	—	2	**3** ←	—	4	—	5	**6** ←	—	**7**	—	1

Notice the difference where the half-steps are located and the tendencies shown by the arrows. In the minor scale, the arrow on the third scale degree is pointing backward toward the half-step; this lowered third scale degree is a defining characteristic of the minor mode.

Learning a New Scale: Begin learning each scale by playing without any rhythm; listen and adjust fingertips to finely tune each pitch before moving to the next note. Then, add a pulse and learn half and quarter notes, the printed rhythm, and finally add slurs as shown below.

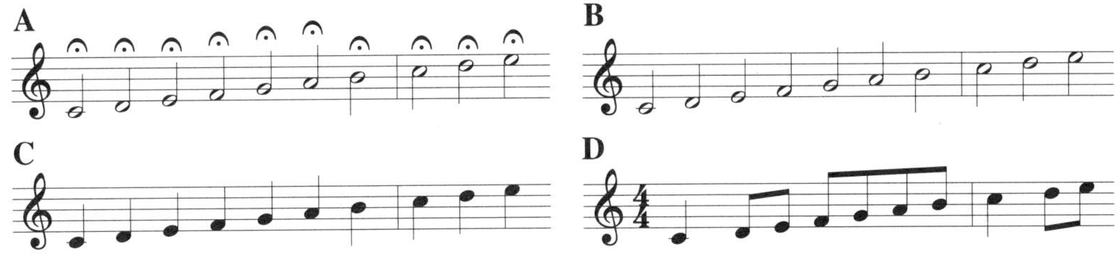

Use the following checklist to guide your practice:

Tone	☐ The **right hand** is relaxed, fingers are curved and in the correct places. ☐ The **bow angle** is perpendicular to the string. ☐ **Bow weight and speed** produce an excellent tone that projects well. ☐ **Contact point** is correctly distanced between bridge and fingerboard.
Intonation	☐ The **instrument** is balanced, and the **left hand** is relaxed and correct. ☐ **Finger patterns**—half-steps and whole-steps—are correct. ☐ **Shifts** are clean and well-executed; **fingerings** are correct. ☐ **Fingertips adjust quickly**, refining the pitch after finger placement.
Rhythm	☐ **Tempos** are consistent; no stopping, stumbling, rushing, or dragging. ☐ Exercise is **memorized** when appropriate.

Major Scales, Arpeggios and Thirds

C Major

scale	C	C♯/D♭	D	D♯/E♭	E	**F**	F♯/G♭	G	G♯/A♭	A	A♯/B♭	**B**	C
degree	1	—	2	—	3	**4** ←	—	5	—	6	—	**7** →	1

G Major

B C C♯ D
E F F♯ G
110. Tuning Canon
1. 2. 3. 4.
111. Tuning Chords
div.
112. One-Octave Scale and Arpeggio
113. Two-Octave Scale and Arpeggio
114. Dominant Arpeggio
x4
115. Thirds
Lower Octave
Upper Octave
scale G G♯/A♭ A A♯/B♭ B C C♯/D♭ D D♯/E♭ E F F♯ G
degree 1 — 2 — 3 4 — 5 — 6 — 7 1

D Major

scale	D	D♯/E♭	E	F	F♯	G	G♯/A♭	A	A♯/B♭	B	C	C♯	D
degree	1	—	2	—	3	**4** ←	—	5	—	6	—	**7** →	1

A Major

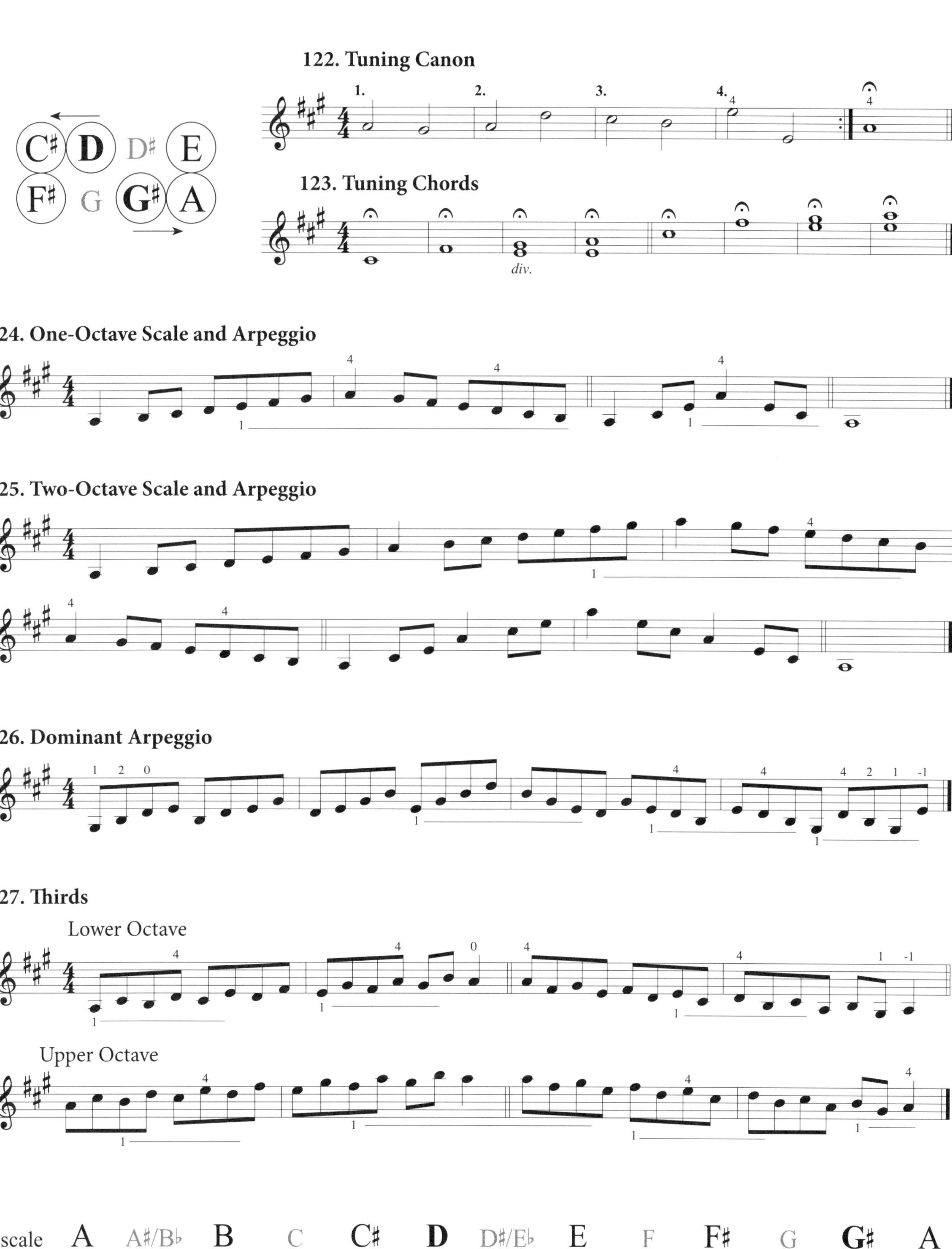

scale	A	A♯/B♭	B	C	C♯	**D**	D♯/E♭	E	F	F♯	G	**G♯**	A
degree	1	—	2	—	3	**4** ←	—	5	—	6	—	**7** →	1

E Major

128. Tuning Canon
1.
2.
3.
4.
G♯ A A♯ B
C♯ D D♯ E
129. Tuning Chords
div.
130. One-Octave Scale and Arpeggio
131. Two-Octave Scale and Arpeggio
132. Dominant Arpeggio
133. Thirds
Lower Octave
Upper Octave
scale E F F♯ G G♯ A A♯/B♭ B C C♯ D D♯ E
degree 1 — 2 — 3 4 — 5 — 6 — 7 1

F Major

scale	F	F♯/G♭	G	G♯/A♭	A	**B♭**	B	C	C♯/D♭	D	D♯/E♭	**E**	F
degree	1	—	2	—	3	**4** ←	—	5	—	6	—	**7** →	1

B♭ Major

143. Two-Octave Scale and Arpeggio

144. Dominant Arpeggio

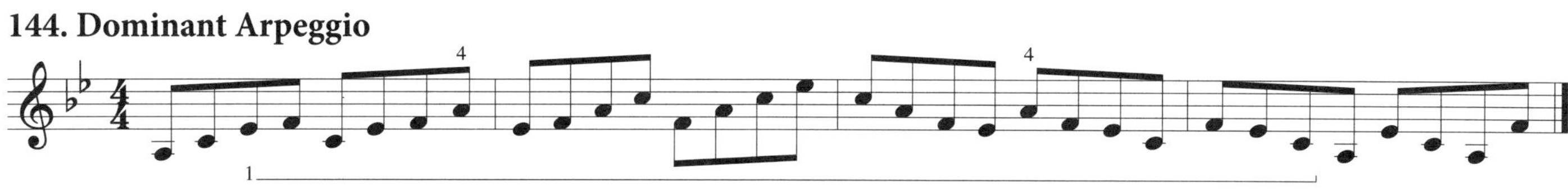

145. Thirds

Lower Octave

scale	B♭	B	C	C♯/D♭	D	E♭	E	F	F♯/G♭	G	G♯/A♭	A	B♭
degree	1	—	2	—	3	4 ←	—	5	—	6	—	7 →	1

E♭ Major

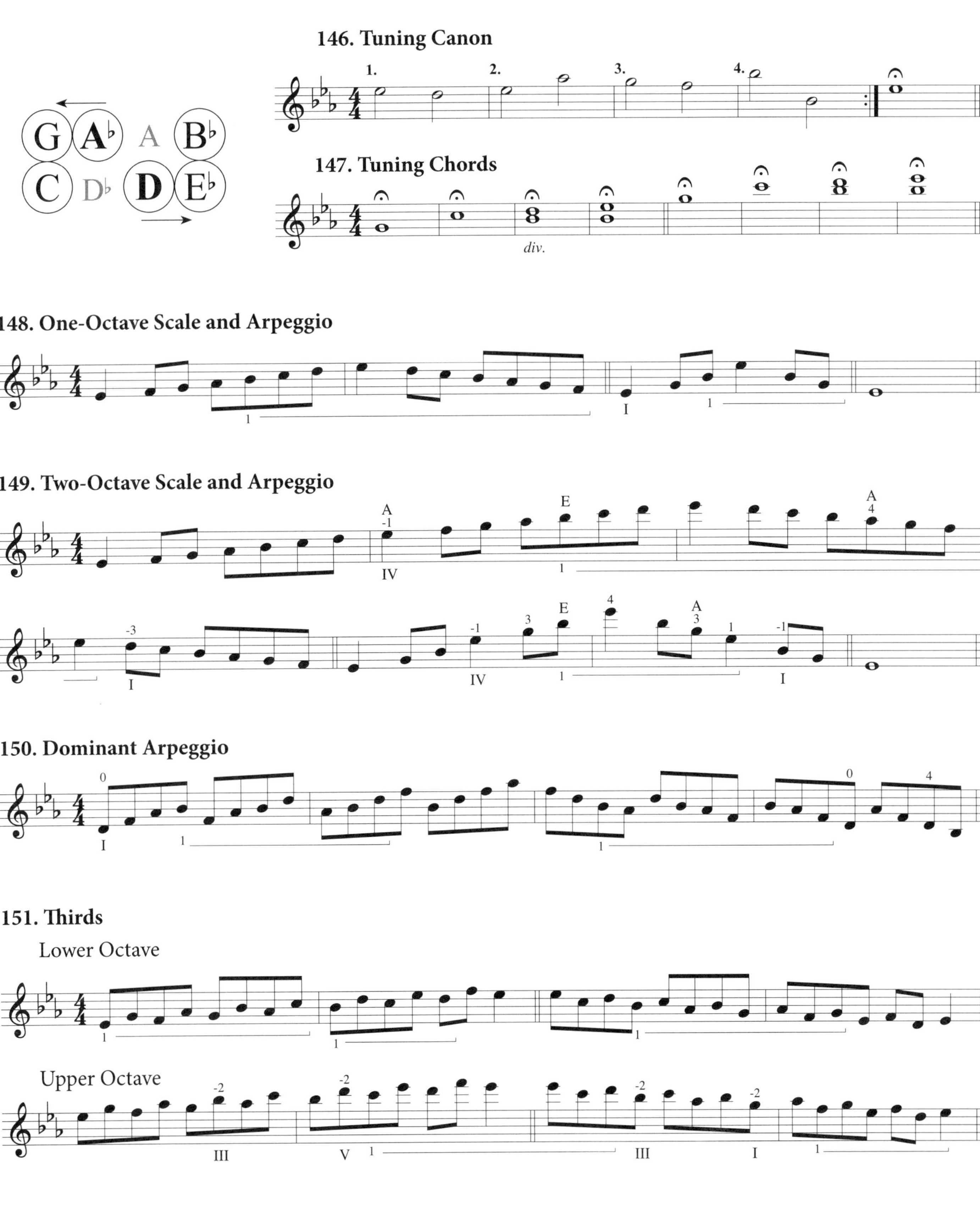

scale	E♭	E	F	F♯/G♭	G	A♭	A	B♭	B	C	C♯/D♭	D	E♭
degree	1	—	2	—	3	4 ←	—	5	—	6	—	7 →	1

A♭ Major

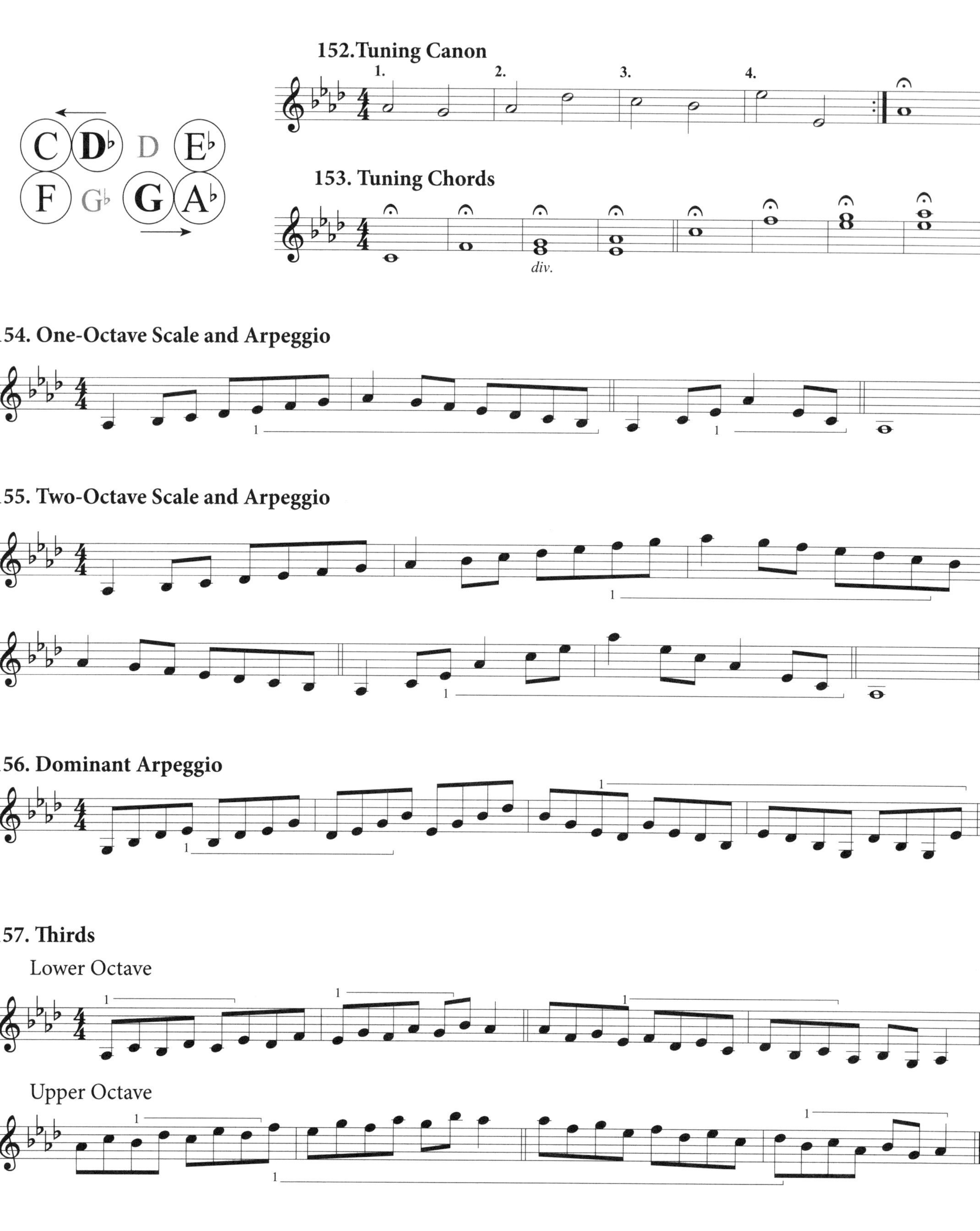

scale	A♭	A	B♭	B	C	D♭	D	E♭	E	F	F♯/G♭	G	A♭
degree	1	—	2	—	3	4	—	5	—	6	—	7	1

Melodic Minor Scales, Arpeggios and Thirds

A Melodic Minor

scale	A	A♯/B♭	B	C♮	C♯/D♭	D	D♯/E♭	E	F♮	F♯/G♭	G	G♯/A♭	A
degree	1	—	2	**3**	—	4	—	5	**6**	—	**7**	—	1

D Melodic Minor

G Melodic Minor

C Melodic Minor

scale	C	C♯/D♭	D	E♭	E	F	F♯/G♭	G	A♭	A	B♭	B	C
degree	1	—	2	**3**	—	4	—	5	**6**	—	**7**	—	1

F Melodic Minor

E Melodic Minor

B Melodic Minor

F♯ Melodic Minor

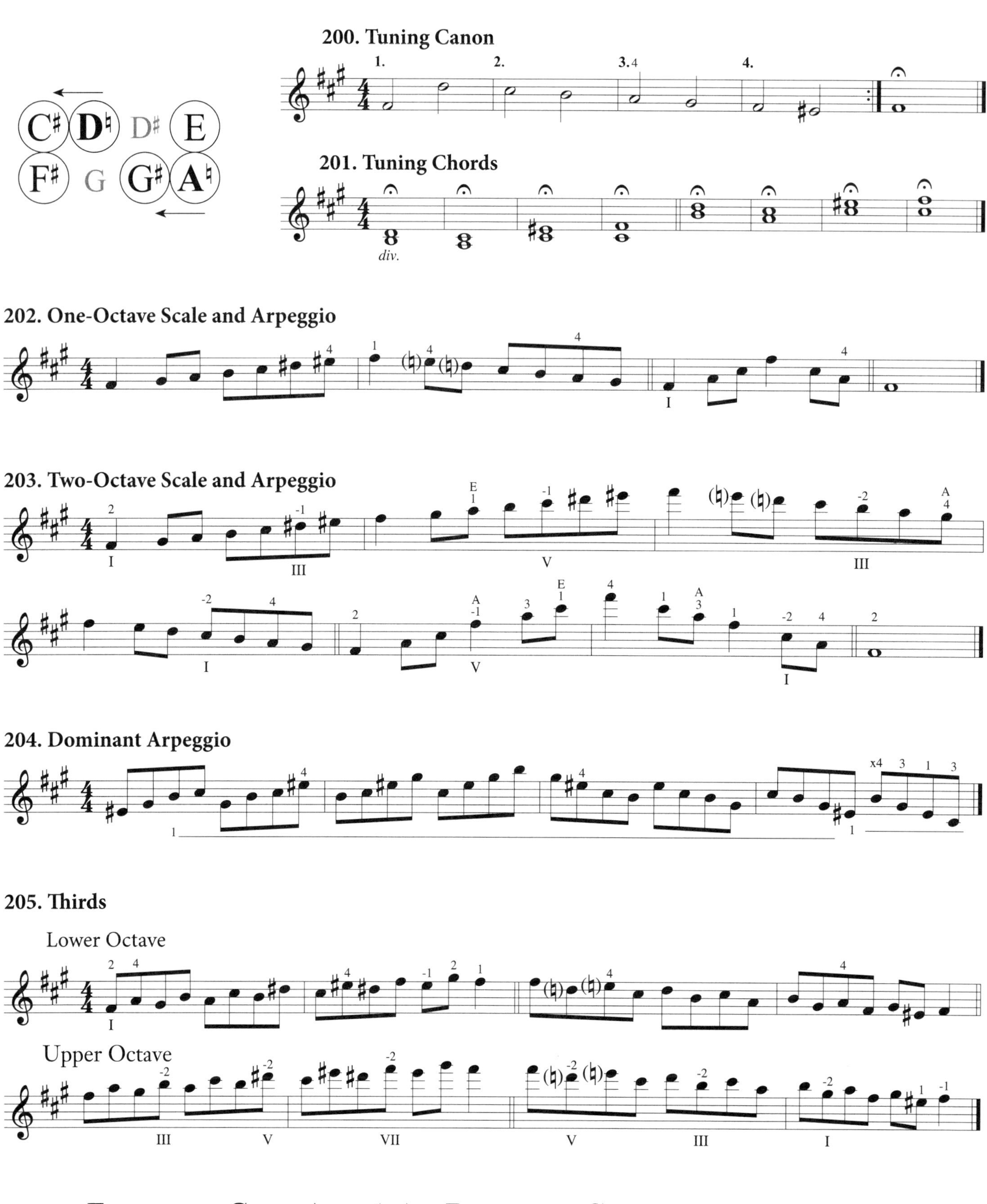

scale	F♯	G	G♯	A	A♯/B♭	B	C	C♯	D	D♯/E♭	E	F	F♯
degree	1	—	2	**3** ←	—	4	—	5	**6** ←	—	**7**	—	1

C♯ Melodic Minor

scale	C♯	D	D♯	E	F	F♯	G	G♯	A	A♯/B♭	B	C	C♯
degree	1	—	2	3	—	4	—	5	6	—	7	—	1

V Chorales

212. Chorale #1

Violin I

213. Chorale #2

Violin I

214. Chorale #3

Violin I

215. Chorale #4

Violin I

216. Chorale #5

Violin I

212. Chorale #1

213. Chorale #2

214. Chorale #3

215. Chorale #4

216. Chorale #5

217. Chorale #6

218. Chorale #7

219. Chorale #8

220. Chorale #9

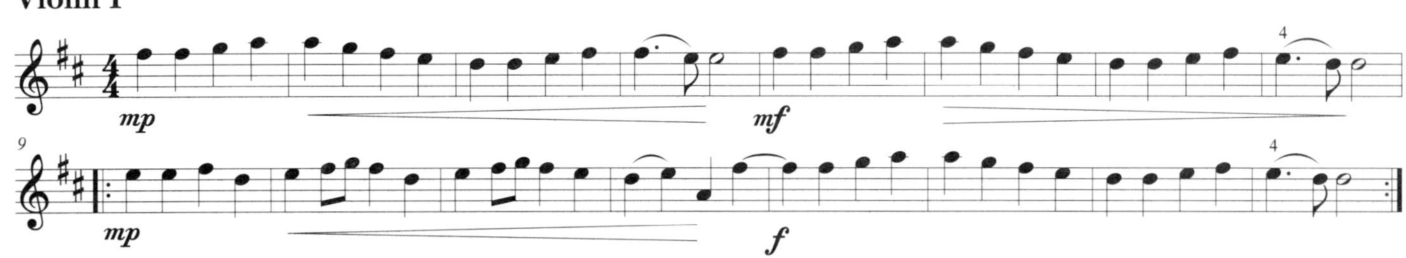

217. Chorale #6

Violin II

218. Chorale #7

Violin II

219. Chorale #8

Violin II

220. Chorale #9

Violin II

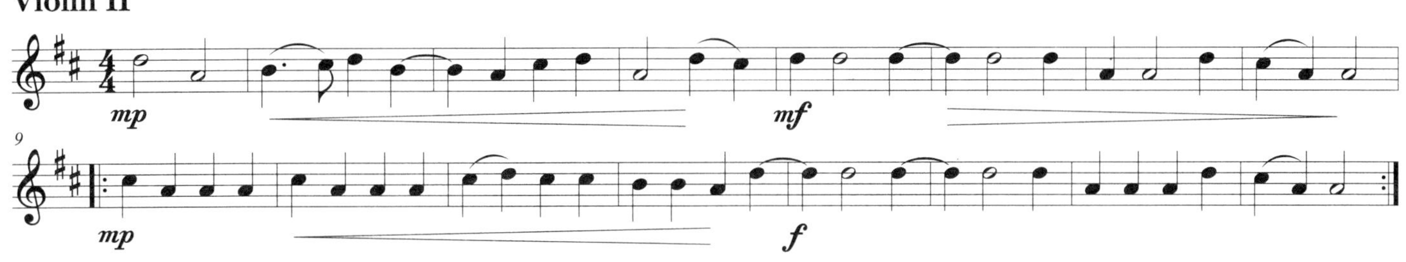

221. Chorale #10

Violin I

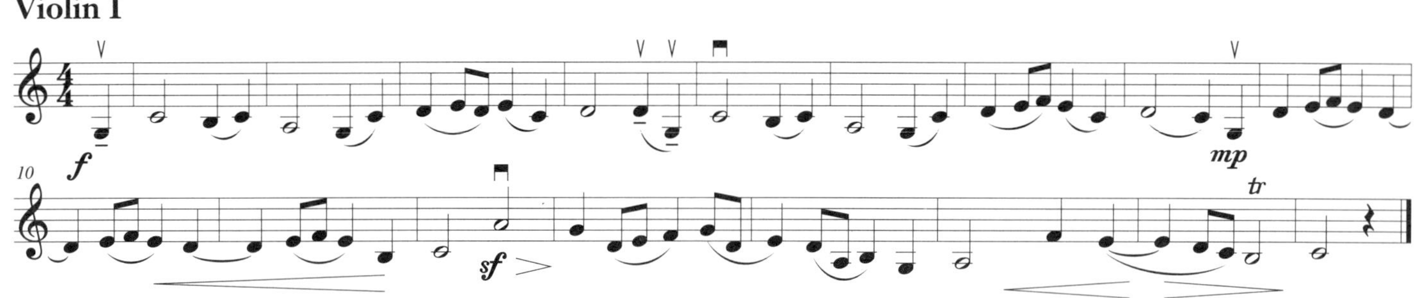

222. Chorale #11

Violin I

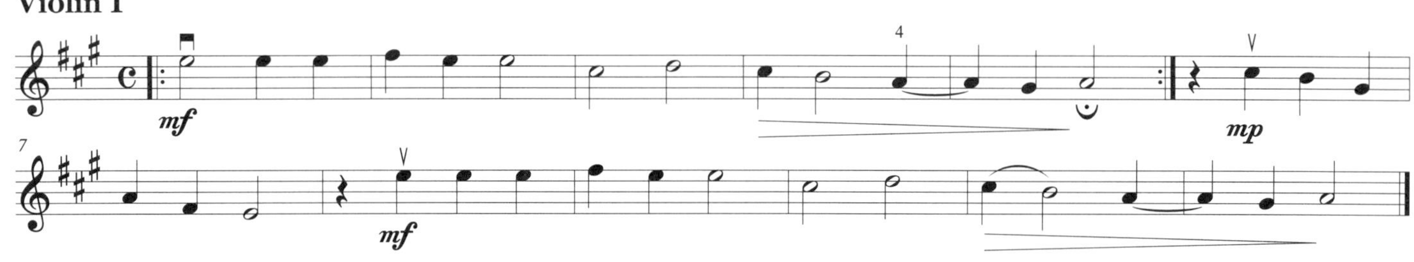

223. Chorale #12

Violin I

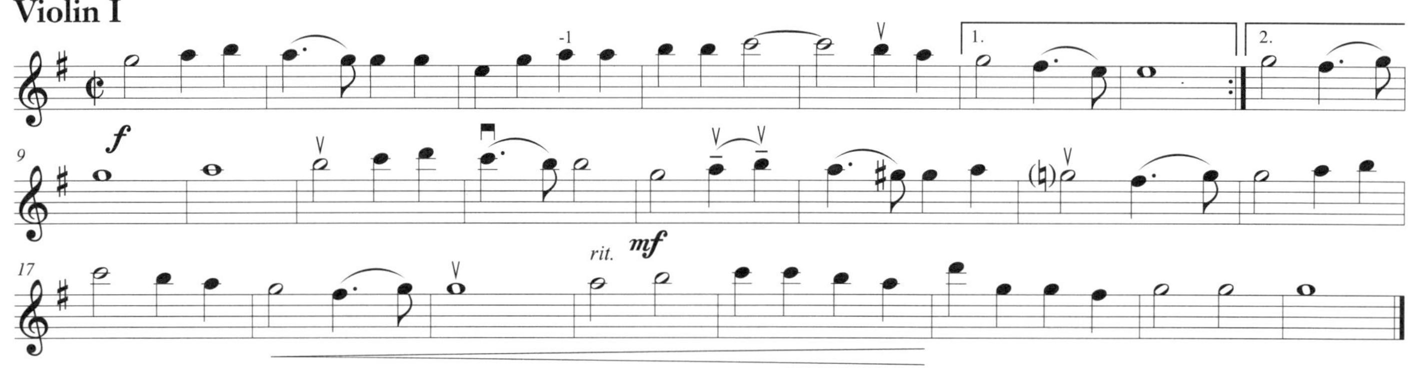

224. Chorale #13

Violin I

221. Chorale #10

Violin II

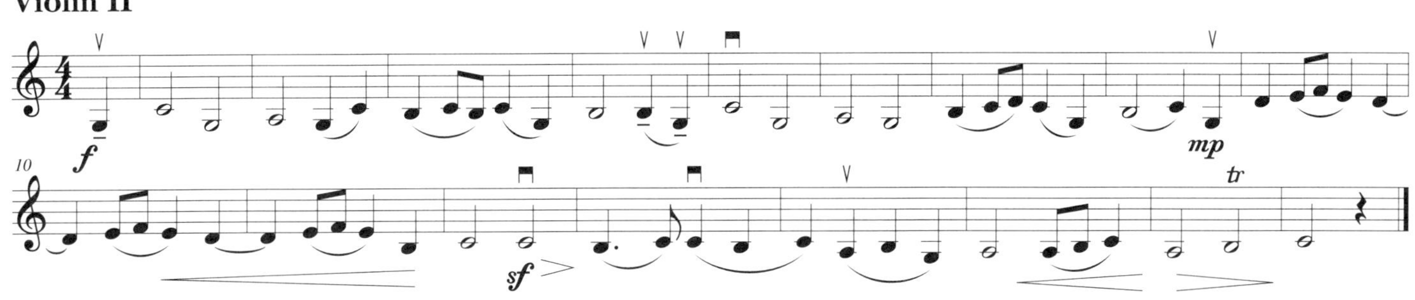

222. Chorale #11

Violin II

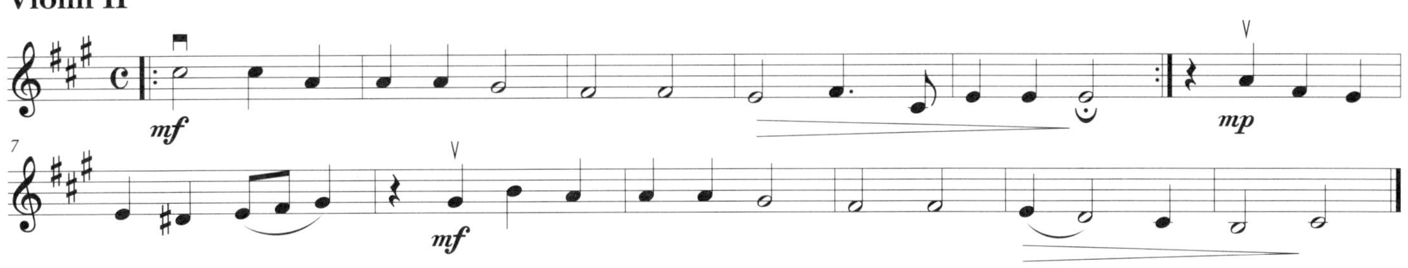

223. Chorale #12

Violin II

224. Chorale #13

Violin II

225. Chorale #14

225. Chorale #14

Violin II

VI Rhythm Vocabulary

A. Quarter Notes and Rests; Eighth Notes

All rhythm has two components: the pulse and the rhythm that goes over the pulse. To genuinely understand a rhythm pattern, students must perform the rhythm while simultaneously keeping a consistent pulse somewhere else in their body. Students MUST count while performing a rhythm with their body or instrument.

For additional practice with quarter notes and rests, go to Part VII Sight Reading Exercises 280–287.

B. Eighth Rests

231.

232.

233.

234.

235.

For additional practice with eighth rests, go to Part VII Sight Reading Exercises 288–295.

C. Ties

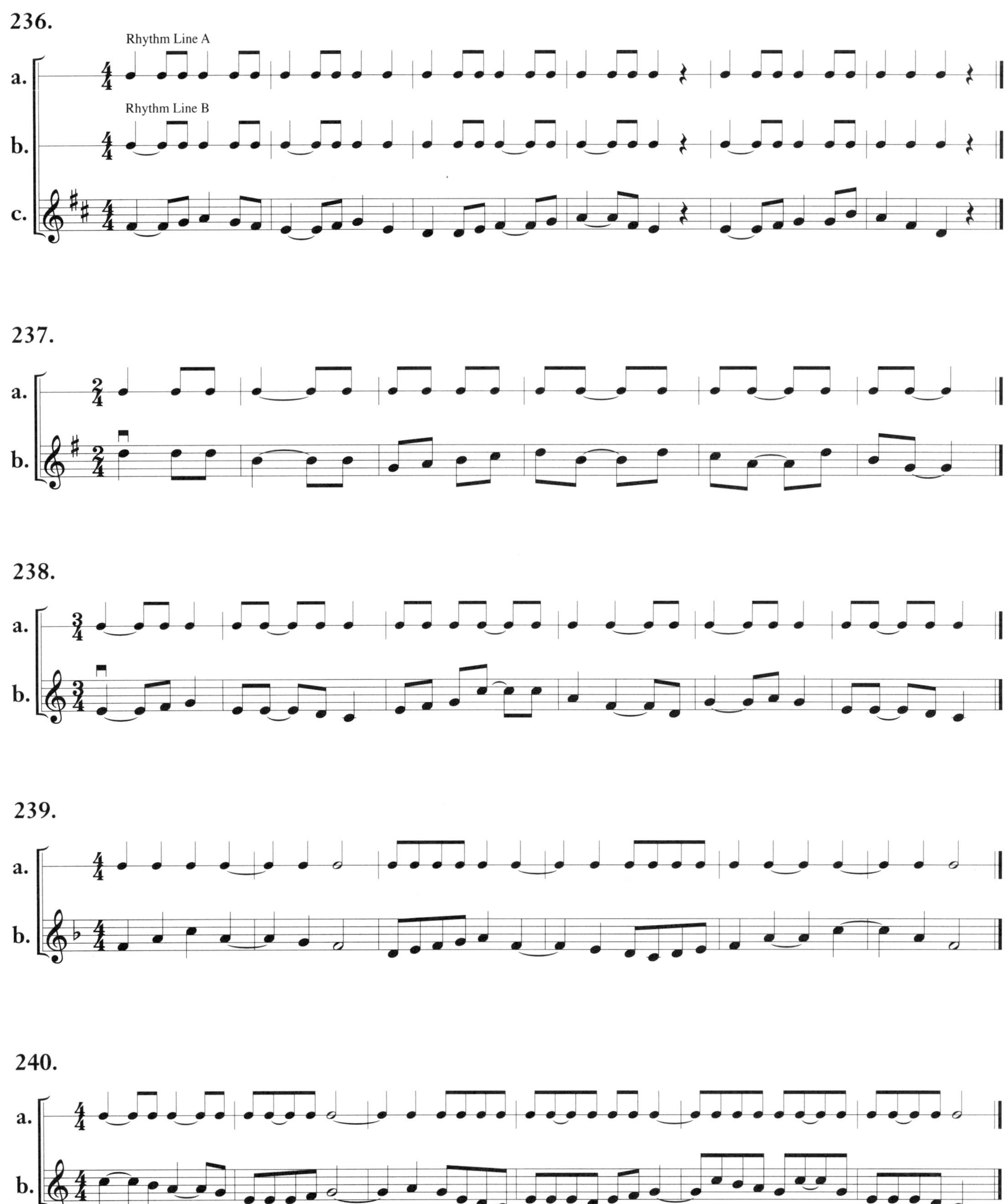

For additional practice with ties, go to Part VII Sight Reading Exercises 296–303.

D. Dotted Quarter Notes

For additional practice with dotted quarter notes, go to Part VII Sight Reading Exercises 304–310.

E. Syncopation

For additional practice with syncopation, go to Part VII Sight Reading Exercises 311–317.

F. Eighth Notes in Compound Meters

For additional practice with eighth notes in compound meters, go to Part VII Sight Reading Exercises 318–325.

G. Sixteenth Notes in Simple Meters

For additional practice with sixteenth notes in simple meters, go to Part VII Sight Reading Exercises 326–334.

H. Sixteenth Notes in Compound Meters

261.

262.

263.

264.

For additional practice with sixteenth notes in compound meters, go to Part VII Sight Reading Exercises 335–342.

I. Dotted Eighth-Sixteenth Combinations

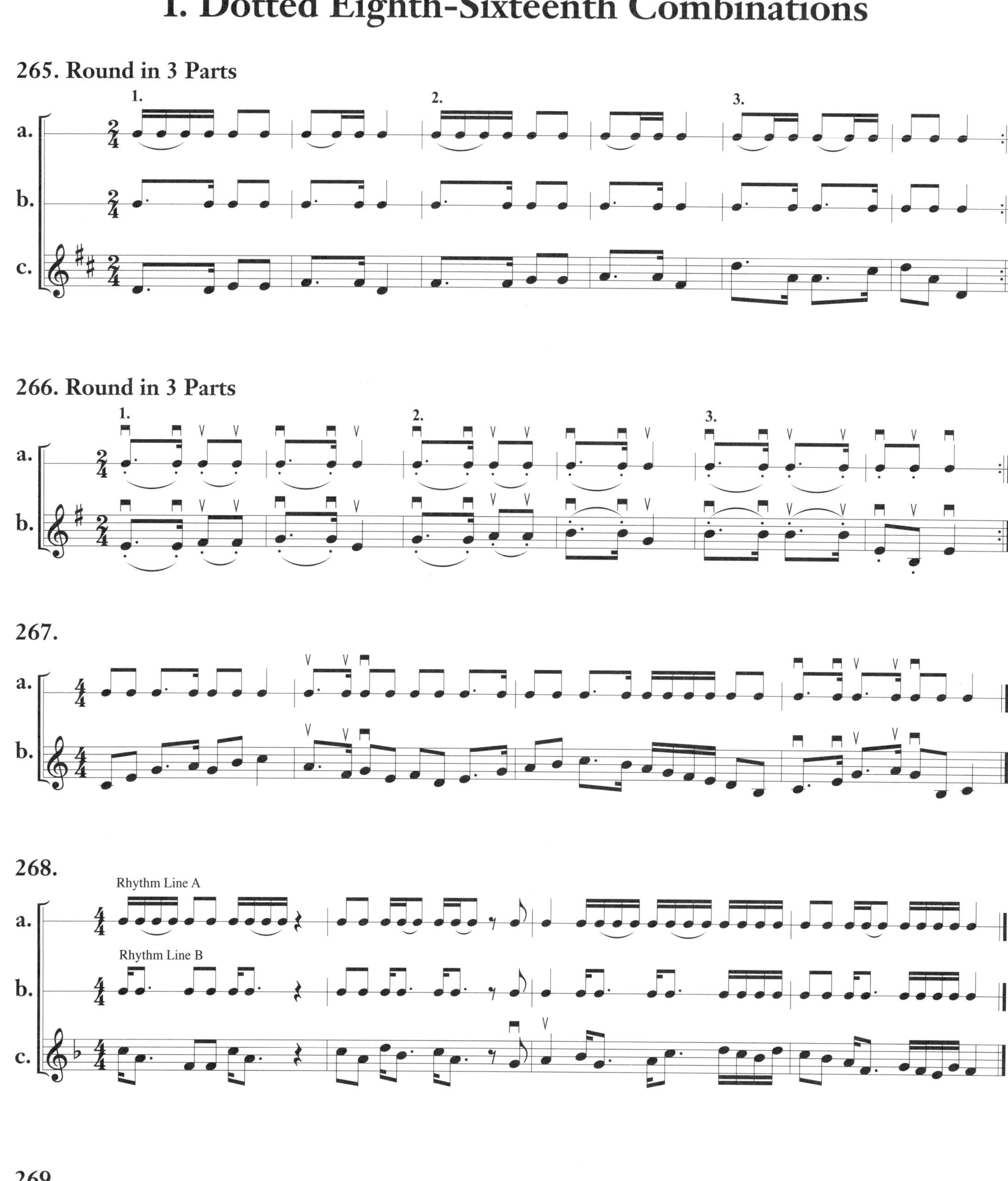

270.

271.

a.

Rhythm Line A

Rhythm Line B

b.

272.

273.

274.

For additional practice with dotted eighth-sixteenth combinations, go to Part VII Sight Reading Exercises 343–351.

J. Triplets

For additional practice with triplets, go to Part VII Sight Reading Exercises 352–360.

VII Sight Reading

A. Quarter Notes and Eighth Notes

B. Eighth Rests

C. Ties

296.
297. Round in 3 Parts
1.
2.
3.
298.
299.
300. Round in 3 Parts
1.
2.
3.
301.
302. Duet
Part A
Part B
303. Duet
Part A
Part B

D. Dotted Quarter Notes

E. Syncopation

F. Eighth Notes in Compound Meters

G. Sixteenth Notes in Simple Meters

H. Sixteenth Notes in Compound Meters

I. Dotted Eighth-Sixteenth Combinations

J. Triplets